The Insect Class

The Insect Class

M A R C   Z A B L U D O F F

 **Marshall Cavendish**
Benchmark
New York

Marshall Cavendish Benchmark
99 White Plains Road
Tarrytown, New York 10591-9001
www.marshallcavendish.us

Library of Congress Cataloging-in-Publication Data

Zabludoff, Marc.
The insect class / by Marc Zabludoff.— 1st ed.
p. cm. — (Family trees)
Includes bibliographical references and index.
ISBN 0-7614-1819-9
1. Insects—Juvenile literature. I. Title. II. Series.

QL467.2.Z324 2005
595.7—dc22

2004021819

Photo research by Linda Sykes Picture Research
Front cover: *Vespula vulgaris,* a common wasp; Title page: Gnat in amber;
Back cover: Leaf-cutting ants

The photographs in this book are used by permission and through the courtesy of:Natural History Museum,
London: Front cover, 10, 16; Darrell Gulin/Corbis: 6; Darwin Dale/Photo Researchers, Inc.: 11 Keith
Eskanos/Picturequest: 14 top right; Picturequest: 14 middle left; Burke/Triolo/Picturequest: 14 middle left; Jeff
Schultz/Alaskan Express/Picturequest: 14 middle right; Martin Ruegner/Imagestate-Pictor/Picturequest: 15
bottom middle; Royalty-Free/Corbis: 14 top left; 14 middle center, 14 bottom left, 15 top right, 15 middle row
(all), 15 bottom left; David Dennis/Animals Animals/Earth Scenes: 15 top left Sea World, Inc./ Corbis: 14 bot-
tom right Swift/Vanuga Images/Corbis: 14 bottom row (middle); Photodisc/Getty Images: 14 bottom right, 15
bottom row, second from right, 15 bottom right; Arthur Siegelman/Visuals Unlimited: 19; James Amos/Photo
Researchers, Inc.: 20; Robert Noonan/Photo Researchers, Inc.: 23; Jerome Wexler/Visuals Unlimited: 24, 61; Jon
Bertsch/Visuals Unlimited: 25; Paul A. Zahal/Photo Researchers, Inc.: 26; Konrad Wothe/Minden Pictures: 28;
James L. Amos/Corbis: 30; Nigel Cattlin/Photo Researchers, Inc.: 32, 57; Gerold and Cynthia Merker/Visuals
Unlimited: 34; Stephen Dalton/Photo Researchers, Inc.: 36, 39, 48, 75; Charles Melton/Visuals Unlimited: 37;
Biophoto Associates/Photo Researchers, Inc.: 38; Scott Camazine/Photo Researchers, Inc.: 41, 47; Eye of
Science/Photo Researchers, Inc.: 43; Dr. Dennis Kunkel/Visuals Unlimited:44; SPL/Photo Researchers, Inc.: 46;
John Gerlach/Visuals Unlimited: 49; Frans Lanting/Minden Pictures: 50; David Wrobel/Visuals Unlimited: 52;
Visuals Unlimited: 53; Ken Thomas/Photo Researchers, Inc.: 55; Peter Johnson/Corbis: 59; Martin
Harvey/Peter Arnold, Inc.: 63; Anthony Bannister/Gallo Images/Corbis: 64; Leroy Simon/Visuals Unlimited:
66; Cisca Castelijns/Foto Natura/Minden Pictures: 70; George D. Lepp/Corbis: 71; Joe McDonald/Visuals
Unlimited: 73, 76; Stepehen J. Krasemann/Photo Researchers, Inc.: 74; Dr. Thomas Eisner: 77; Dr. John
Alcock/Visuals Unlimited: 78; Valorie Hodgson/Visuals Unlimited: 79; Ray Coleman/Visuals Unlimited: 81;
Reuters/Corbis: 83; Chris Rogers/Corbis: 85; Royalty-Free/Corbis: back cover

Printed in Malaysia

Book design by Patrice Sheridan

1 3 5 6 4 2

C O N T E N T S

Insects exist in a variety far greater than that of any other animal on Earth. There are roughly 20,000 different species of butterfly alone.

A World of Insects

Insects have been here a lot longer than humans—at least several hundred million years longer. They also vastly outnumber not only us, but us lumped together with every other animal on Earth. So far, scientists have identified and named about 1.5 million different species, or distinct kinds, of animals living on the planet. About a million of them are insects. That list is not complete, though. Animals are still being discovered and named every year. Most of them are small and found in tropical rain forests. Of these, the overwhelming majority—perhaps 10,000 new species a year— are insects. How many insects remain to be found—and how many will go extinct as the rain forests are destroyed—is anyone's guess. Some scientists think there are another million insect species waiting to be discovered. Others think the number is closer to 10 million. Still others are confident that there exist 30 million more species, so far completely unknown to us.

A fair estimate is that insects make up a colossal 80 percent of all animal species on Earth. As to how many individual creeping and burrowing and flying creatures there are, no one knows for sure. One astonishing estimate is that there are as many insects in one square mile (2.6 square km) of Earth's land surface as there are humans on the entire planet. There are more than 6 billion humans worldwide, which means that the United States alone must be home to more than 21,719,814,000,000,000 insects. Rounded off, that is almost 22 quintillion or 22 million billion.

With the exception of the frozen interior of Antarctica, insects cover all the continents in great numbers. They inhabit every field, every forest, every mountain and valley, every desert and plain, every city, and every home.

How can we even begin to make sense of the immense variety of these six-legged creatures?

THE SEARCH FOR ORDER

Humans have probably always tried to impose some order on the things they find around them. It seems to be the way our mind works. At the very least, order helps us find something when we need it: phone numbers in a phone book, books in a library, the right seats at a concert.

To sort out the stuff in our homes we use simple rules. We arrange books alphabetically or by subject, music by type, food by expiration date. Nature is considerably harder to get a handle on. The world is filled with lions and lichens, flounders and flowers, sponges and spiders and spotted sparrows. Even if you were not interested in science, you might still want to sort those items into groups—which are edible and which are best avoided. If you were curious about the world, you might want to understand which items properly belong together and which do not. Do flounders go with sponges since they both live in the sea? Do lions belong with lichens because they share a fondness for lying around on rocks?

Although such questions have probably occupied human minds for many thousands of years, the first record we have of someone actually trying to figure out the grand scheme of nature comes from ancient Greece. In the fourth century B.C.E. the Greek philosopher Aristotle, after making close observations of more than 500 animals, noted that certain features suggested that some animals were more similar to one another than they were to others. Animals with tusks, he saw, formed a separate group from animals with horns. Animals that gave birth to live young were separate from animals that laid eggs. He was absolutely correct when he claimed that dolphins should be placed with land-dwelling mammals and not with fish. He was only half-right when he decided that, on the basis of their colorless blood, all insects should be grouped with spiders, lobsters, clams, and oysters (the last two are the odd ones in the group).

After Aristotle, no one questioned the idea that there was an organizing principle to nature, a logic that explained why things were as we found them. But few agreed on what the hidden order of nature was. Not until the seventeenth century did anyone take a truly scientific approach to classifying life. In England an intensely curious, hardworking man named John Ray began to make detailed observations of thousands of plants and animals. He was the first to draw relationships between animals based on their overall body shape and design rather just one feature like tusks. He looked at teeth and hooves especially, and began to find common threads linking large groups of familiar creatures.

Ray's cataloging was greatly extended in the eighteenth century by the Swedish scientist Karl von Linné, or Linnaeus, as he is generally known. Linnaeus spent his life sorting plants and animals into what he thought were their proper arrangement. Most importantly for us, Linnaeus established the basic system by which we name and classify all living things today.

Linnaeus started with the nearly obvious recognition that animals belonged to certain basic types that did not mix with each other. Brown squirrels always produced more brown squirrels, not chipmunks. These fundamental types he called species. Species, he saw, were sometimes very similar to one another. House cats and lions, for example, were quite alike in general appearance and structure, despite their difference in size. Such similar species, he said, could be grouped into a broader category called a genus. Likewise, similar genera (plural of *genus*) could be gathered into a still broader group called a family.

With at least 300,000 separate species—about one-fifth of all animal species—beetles pose a huge challenge for scientists who try to arrange them in appropriate groups.

Even the familiar firefly comes in an astonishing number of forms: about 2,000 species, divided among three different families.

He continued this process, adding the even broader categories of class and order. Each of these categories was called a taxon, and so the science of classification is known as taxonomy. Linnaeus also established the method of naming that is known as binomial nomenclature. Each organism was described by two names, a genus name and a species name, both of which were in Latin.

The choice of language made sense. First of all, at the time, Latin was the language of educated people throughout the Western world. With Latin, a scientist in Sweden could easily correspond with a scientist in

The Many Levels of Classification

Organisms are classified based on how they can be grouped into the different levels of taxonomical classification. In levels below the class Insecta, insects can be grouped according to their wing structure, body structure, or other physical characteristics. For example, the Hymenoptera order includes insects with membrane wings.

This is how a honeybee would be classified:

Kingdom:	Animalia (all the animals)
Phylum:	Arthropoda (animals with jointed legs, segmented bodies, and an exoskeleton)
Class:	Insecta (all the insects)
Order:	Hymenoptera (insects with "membrane wings")
Family:	Apidae (bees)
Genus:	*Apis* (honeybees)
Species:	*mellifera* (European honeybee)

By tradition, genus names are capitalized, and both the genus name and species name are in italics, so the honeybee's scientific name is *Apis mellifera.*

France. Second, different cultures used different common names for creatures. Even in English-speaking countries there are beetles known variously as ladybirds or ladybugs and lightning bugs or fireflies. Without one agreed-upon scientific name, how could two scientists ever be certain they were referring to the same animal?

Scientists after Linnaeus extended the taxonomy system, adding the even broader categories of phylum and kingdom. Today, most scientists agree that there are five kingdoms of life: animals, plants, fungi, bacteria, and protoctists (mostly single-celled organisms). There is some disagreement on how many phyla (plural of *phylum*) there are—somewhere between twenty and thirty. A phylum represents a basic design that is fundamentally different from all others. Earthworms are in one phylum, for instance, while starfish are in another and animals with a backbone in yet another.

With this system in place, we can begin to get a handle on the immense variety of insects in our world.

Scientists classify living things in arrangements like this family tree of the an[...]

A N I M[...]

PHYLA

CNIDARIANS

Coral

ARTHROPODS

(Animals with external skeletons and jointed limbs)

MOLLUSKS

Octopus

SUB PHYLA

CLASSES

CRUSTACEANS

Lobster

ARACHNIDS

Spider

INSECTS

Butterfly

MYRIAPODS

Centipede

ORDERS

CARNIVORES

Bear

SEA MAMMALS
(2 ORDERS)

Dolphin

PRIMATES

Monkey

dom to highlight the connections and the differences among the many forms of life.

N G D O M

ANNELIDS

Earthworm

CHORDATES

(Animals
with a
dorsal
nerve chord)

ECHINODERMS

Starfish

VERTEBRATES

(Animals
with a
backbone)

FISH

Fish

BIRDS

Penguin

MAMMALS

AMPHIBIANS

Frog

REPTILES

Snake

HERBIVORES
(5 ORDERS)

Horse

RODENTS

Squirrel

INSECTIVORES

Hedgehog

MARSUPIALS

Kangaroo

SMALL MAMMALS
(SEVERAL ORDERS)

Rabbit

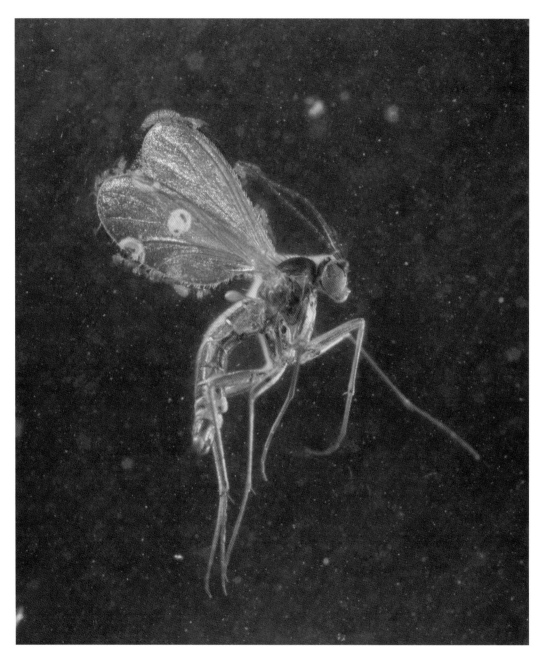

Some of our best insect fossils are of creatures encased in amber, a hardened form of tree sap. This perfectly preserved fungus gnat is 40 million years old.

Insects with Class

We can ultimately trace the whole splendid variety of insect life back to sometime between 3.5 and 4 billion years ago. Scientists project that is when all life on Earth got its start, in the form of single-celled bacteria. But it was not until around 550 million years ago that recognizable animals began scuttling around the bottom of the seas. Among them were the ancestors of all arthropods, one of the major divisions of the animal kingdom.

The phylum Arthropoda contains all animals that have jointed legs (the Greek word *arthro* means "joint"), that have bodies divided into numerous ringlike segments, and that protect those bodies with an exo-, or "outside," skeleton. Four large groups of animals alive today share these basic characteristics, and they are:

- The crustaceans, such as lobsters, crabs, and shrimps, most of which live in the sea, and all of which have five pairs of legs;
- The arachnids, a group whose members include spiders, scorpions, ticks, and mites, all of which have four pairs of legs (and all of which are not insects);
- The myriapods (literally, the "ten thousand feet"), which include all the centipedes and millipedes (they are not insects either);

- The insects, members of the class Insecta, all of which, by the time they are adults, have three pairs of legs.

To be an insect, an animal must possess two essential characteristics. First, it must have a body divided into three main sections. (*Insect* and *section* both come from the Latin word *secare,* meaning "to cut into.") The three sections are a head; a middle, called a thorax; and an abdomen. Second, it must have, in the adult stage, only six legs. Most of the time, although not always, it will also have wings. But the three body sections and the three pairs of legs are an absolute requirement. That is why spiders and centipedes do not make the cut.

For more than 100 million years, the ancestors of all these arthropods were content to live in the sea, along with all other forms of life. But around 400 million years ago, some of them began leaving their watery home to try living on the land. Until shortly before then the land had been a barren place. But it was being carpeted by green as the first land plants began to take hold. Right behind the plants marched—or more likely, crawled—the arthropods. Among these first explorers were some whose descendants would soon become spiders and scorpions as well as others whose descendants would become insects.

Who exactly were these pioneering arthropods? Unfortunately we do not know, and there is a good chance that we never will. Small and delicate creatures do not easily survive, even as fossils. Whatever rock-hard impressions of these insect ancestors might have existed may well have been pulverized over the hundreds of millions of years that passed before any humans appeared to look for them.

What we do know is that the insects evolved quickly. Rare fossils found in Scotland show that by 380 million years ago, animals that looked extremely like springtails, arthropods that still thrive today, were crawling about. Today, tiny, dark springtails can be found under the moist leaves and vegetation surrounding any pond or lake or lining the floor of any forest. Their name comes from their powerful springlike tail, which they use

Springtails, which use their tails to "hop," are often considered the most primitive insects. They do not look much different from their 380-million-year-old ancestors.

to "hop" when in need of a quick escape. Springtails are often considered to be the most primitive insects. They have no wings—as certainly the first insects did not, either—but they do have six legs.

Over the next few tens of millions of years, different forms of insects began appearing rapidly. By 330 million years ago, cockroaches were scurrying across forest floors. Dragonflies were darting through the treetops. Some insects were far larger than their modern descendants. This period, called the Carboniferous, was the only time that insects tried out large size as a strategy for success. Dragonflies grew as large as a modern seagull; one fossil shows a wingspan of 30 inches (76 cm). Insects were not the only creatures of the day to test the advantages of bigness. Millipedes of the Carboniferous grew to an astonishing 6.5 feet (2 m). No one is sure why animals of this time went to such unusual lengths. However, some scientists think that higher oxygen levels in the atmosphere had something to do with it.

Fossils reveal that dragonflies can trace their family back more than 300 million years. They were among Earth's earliest flying predators

By 300 million years ago the ancestors of today's grasshoppers had appeared (although Earth had no grass yet), along with ancestors of katydids and crickets and cicadas. These early insects were likely the first Earthly makers of musical sounds. Hundreds of millions of years before the first bird would ever sing, the familiar calls of these insects floated through the ancient forests of Earth.

Within another 100 million years, nearly all the modern orders of insects had appeared, representing not just crickets and cockroaches but also beetles, flies, lice, mantises, bees, wasps, ants, moths, and butterflies. It is not yet clear precisely when the termites showed up—their fossils do not appear until much later. Indeed, it is likely that many of these insect groups evolved earlier; we just do not yet have the fossil evidence to say so with certainty. What we do know is that all these groups were perfectly suited to take advantage of the next great event in evolutionary history: the appearance of the first flowering plants.

TIMELINE OF INSECT ORIGINS

Origin of insects

400 MYA ———

Oldest fossil insects (springtails)

360 ———

First winged insects

Evolution of metamorphosis
    Appearance of mayflies and ancestral dragonflies

Evolution of wing folding
    First appearance of cockroaches
    Appearance of grasshoppers, locusts, crickets, and katydids

285 ———

Appearance of orders representing lice, true bugs, beetles,
    and true flies among others

245 ———

Appearance of stick insects and leaf insects
Appearance of wasps, bees, and ants

210 ———

Appearance of butterflies and moths

145 ———

Origin of flowering plants
    First fossil appearance of termites and fleas

65 ——— **Extinction of dinosaurs**

MYA=million years ago

The Orders of Insects

Just how many orders of insects there are in the class Insecta depends on who is doing the ordering. Some entomologists prefer splitting one order into two, others believe two should be combined into one. Also, some entomologists believe that some of the most ancient insects, such as springtails, are not quite insects after all. Although these animals have six legs, they have other body features and a method of reproduction that sets them apart from all the other members of the class. To show the creatures' more distant relationship to insects, these entomologists put them into separate groups of their own. They, together with the insects, all fit within the superclass Hexapoda, a category containing all "six-footed" arthropods. (Taxonomists often add levels of classification by using the prefixes super-, for "above," and sub-, for "below." A superclass is tucked in just above class; a suborder is set right below order.)

In general, however, there are between twenty-five and thirty-two orders of insects, with perhaps sixteen to twenty major ones. One new order, Mantophasmatodea, was just added in 2002 to accommodate an insect found living in Namibia. The members of this rare order are described as meat-eating combinations of crickets, mantises, and stick insects.

INSECTS AND PLANTS

Flowering plants, called angiosperms, first appeared around 130 million years ago (in the early Cretaceous). We usually think of our planet at that time as dominated by great dinosaurs. But vastly outnumbering the dinosaurs were the insects. They were greedily lapping up the nectar the new flowering plants produced.

Caterpillars—the larvae of butterflies and moths—are essentially eating machines. A large outbreak of these gypsy moth caterpillars can devastate local plant populations.

The history of insects and the history of plants are woven together so tightly that scientists often refer to these two groups as a perfect example of "co-evolution." The two groups depend heavily on each other, and changes in one always cause changes in the other. But insects and plants do not have a straightforward, loving relationship. From the very beginning, they have both needed each other and sought to destroy each other.

The earliest insects got their nourishment from a steady diet of plants. For more than 200 million years, insects sucked up the plants' sap, nibbled on their spores and fruits, and chewed on their stems and leaves. If plants had not come up with some defense against the insects, they would have been eaten out of existence. Early plants and trees tried out various strategies. Some trees grew cones to surround and protect their seeds. Some plants became poisonous. Others grew leaves coated with tiny hairs or slicked with oil to make it harder for six-legged diners to grab hold. (Many of the herbs we use today, like basil, evolved their oils for insect defense.)

Usually insects prey on plants, but sometimes the tables are turned. This sundew plant uses sticky droplets to trap insects for food.

Insects responded with tricks of their own. Beetles developed tougher, stronger mouths; flies became better, higher fliers. A whole army of insects grew longer legs or shorter legs, flatter bodies or narrower bodies, all in an attempt to get the protein-rich food the plants provided.

After a couple hundred million years of this, some plants hit upon the clever device of using insects rather than fighting them. Plants, like animals, reproduce sexually. To produce offspring, a female egg cell must be fertilized by a male sperm cell. Early plants let the wind carry away a multitude of their spores as a way to bring a few eggs and sperm together. But by 130 million years ago, some plants began to enlist insects to do the job for them. They enticed them with irresistible smells, juicy fruits, and, eventually, flowers. All were designed to attract insects to come drink from the plants' well of sugary nectar and in return carry away some pollen to another plant.

Many flowering plants such as the bee orchid have evolved to depend on specific insect species to carry their pollen from one plant to another.

The appearance of flowering plants also seems to have spurred the development of complicated behavior among some insects. This is when the complex societies of ants and bees first started, with different members of the nest or hive assigned to different, specialized tasks. Exactly what the steps were that led from flowers to "social insects" is not precisely clear. But it seems certain that the two were linked.

FOSSILS

How do we know anything at all about this long-ago history? For the most part, our knowledge comes from the evidence preserved as fossils.

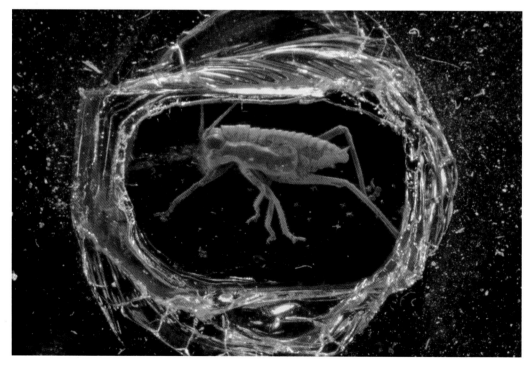

The amber that surrounds this grasshopper was once sticky sap, a defensive weapon developed by a tree to guard itself against insect diners.

The gentle impressions of insects buried in sand or silt and gradually turned into rock leave us with an astonishing, though sketchy, picture of ancient life. Insect bodies are so fragile that few ever survived as fossils. But fortunately, enough have survived to give us a pretty good idea of their evolution.

We can see preserved in rock the wings of a dragonfly that flew through a real Jurassic park. We can study the body of a roach that scurried across a forest floor millions of years before the first dinosaur footstep. We can even see the color pattern on the wings of an insect from 275 million years ago.

But some of our most spectacular fossils come not from rock but from amber. Amber is most often encountered today in the form of deep-yellow beads. But it was once a thick, syrupy sap that oozed out of trees similar to pines. Every so often a careless insect was trapped in the sticky stuff and slowly encased in a transparent yellow coffin. Over millions of years that resin dried and hardened. Sealed inside the amber are the bodies of these trapped insects, exquisitely preserved in all their glorious detail. From a few famous amber deposits around the world—in northern Europe, Lebanon, and New Jersey—we have a spectacular record of insects from the last great age of the dinosaurs.

All insect bodies are divided into three sections, but they can exhibit a huge number of variations. The giraffe weevil's elongated thorax is among the most extreme

The Physical Insect

All insect bodies are similar enough that we can talk about them in general, as a unified group. But it is important to keep in mind that when we are describing the body of a typical insect, we are not describing the body of any insect in particular. Insects show up in a huge assortment of shapes, sizes, and adornments.

A R M O R   O N   T H E   O U T S I D E

The insect body is in some ways an inside-out version of our own. An insect's skeleton surrounds the body, and the muscles are attached to its inside surface. Like armor, the exoskeleton of an insect consists of stiff plates, which are made of a substance called chitin. For its weight, chitin is stronger than bone, and at the scale of an insect it offers terrific support.

Between the plates are unstiffened sections that act as joints and allow the animal to move. The plates do not really lie flat on the body. The exoskeleton dips and folds inward in spots to give additional support where it is needed. It also serves as the body's gatekeeper, letting some substances in and keeping others out. For example, the exoskeleton is pierced with tiny pores that allow oxygen to come inside to the insect's tissues. It is also covered with a waxy, waterproof film that keeps the insect from drying out. Many insects' chitin armor can also help with flight. The chitin is stiff, but it is also springy. By squeezing the naturally springy thorax, insects get their wings (attached to the thorax) to bounce up and down a few extra times without using any extra muscle action.

But there is one major disadvantage to living inside a stiff suit of armor: it does not grow as the soft body within it does. At some point the insect must toss away its old armored skin and grow a roomier one. All insects, and all their arthropod relatives, go through this process, called molting, several times during their lives.

The great disadvantage of an exoskeleton is that it can't grow. All insects, therefore, like this cicada, must occasionally shed their too-tight armor for a larger size.

30

FROM END TO END

That growing arthropod body is made up of rings, or segments, linked together end to end—a centipede's body is a good example of a segmented arthropod. An insect's body has about twenty such segments, but many of them may be fused together so that we cannot see each one separately. All insects have those segments grouped into the three main body divisions of head, thorax, and abdomen.

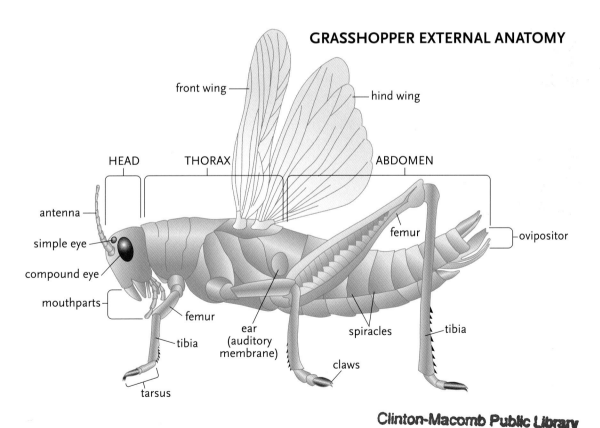

GRASSHOPPER EXTERNAL ANATOMY

front wing — — hind wing

HEAD   THORAX   ABDOMEN

antenna

simple eye

compound eye

mouthparts

femur

femur — ovipositor

tibia

tibia

ear (auditory membrane)

spiracles

claws

tarsus

31

The Head

The insect head is the part most easily understood by us, since it corresponds so nicely to our notion of what a head should be. It is at the front end of the body, it houses the brain, and it is dotted with organs for sensing the world around it—eyes and antennae, mainly. It also provides a convenient spot for the mouth.

An insect's mouth—more precisely, its collection of "mouthparts"—is somewhat harder to understand since it is so unlike our mammal version. In general, the mouth is formed by two jaws, called mandibles, that have sharp serrated edges (like a steak knife) to do the necessary slicing or biting. Unlike our jaws, which move up and down, an insect's mandibles move horizontally, from the sides. Behind the mandibles are a pair of "assistant" jaws, called maxillae, which hold and turn the food and help push it down the throat.

Attached to the maxillae are a pair of fingerlike parts called palps. The palps both handle and taste the food, testing it before it is taken into the body. Covering all these parts is a kind of upper lip, called a labrum, and a lower lip, called a labium. The labium too has a pair of palps, to help move the food around.

A Chinese oak silk moth caterpillar shows off its leaf-munching mouthparts. When caterpillars become nectar-sipping adults, their mouthparts change drastically.

INSECT MOUTHPARTS

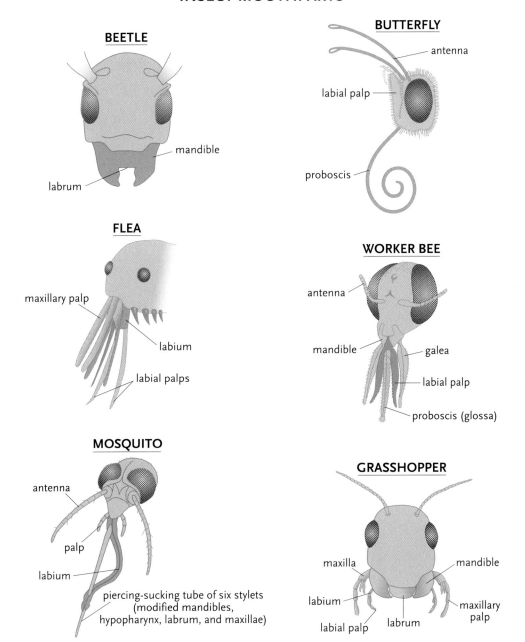

BEETLE

mandible

labrum

BUTTERFLY

antenna

labial palp

proboscis

FLEA

maxillary palp

labium

labial palps

WORKER BEE

antenna

mandible

galea

labial palp

proboscis (glossa)

MOSQUITO

antenna

palp

labium

piercing-sucking tube of six stylets
(modified mandibles,
hypopharynx, labrum, and maxillae)

GRASSHOPPER

maxilla

mandible

labium

maxillary palp

labial palp

labrum

Different types of insects have specialized mouthparts that help them chew or drink their food.

All these mouthparts appear in different forms in different insects. For example, the mandible of a butterfly or moth is a long, hollow tube called a proboscis. It is used for sucking nectar from deep within a flower. This tube is so long that it must be coiled up when not in use. Fleas, meanwhile, have turned their labium, the lower lip, into a sharp pointed skin-piercing instrument.

The Thorax

The thorax, the insect's middle, is made of three segments, with two legs attached to each. The legs have five main sections, each a tube connected to another tube in a ball-and-socket arrangement. Like mouthparts, insect legs vary from one species to the next. Grasshoppers, for example, have

A number of insects, like the painted grasshopper, have a pair of legs greatly modified for some specialized task—in this case, hopping.

hugely enlarged back legs for hopping. Praying mantises have hugely enlarged front legs for grabbing prey.

But a more typical insect, such as an ant, has six legs of about the same size. To get around, insects move those legs in more or less the same way: they move the first and third leg on one side together with the middle leg on the opposite side. Then they switch. This always gives them three feet on the ground—a very stable, triangular arrangement. (We use the same three-foot solution ourselves for things like camera tripods because it gives us something that sits without rocking even when the ground is uneven or the legs are not all quite the same length.) Alternating the two sets of three legs, insects can walk quite well, although in a slight zigzag. And many can run quickly when necessary. Normally, the insect version of running is simply a speeded-up version of their walking pattern, but at times they do surprising things. For example, ants at high speed actually gallop—that is, they get all their legs off the ground at the same time, as horses do. American roaches, when motivated, motor across the floor on only two legs. They run so fast that the front end of their body lifts up off the ground. This gets the roach's shorter front legs out of the way and lets it take bigger steps with its longer rear legs. This neat trick allows the 1.2-inch (30-mm) American cockroach to cover five feet (1.5 m), or 50 body lengths, in a second. To match that performance, a six-foot human would have to run 205 miles per hour (327 kph).

Along with legs, the thorax often sports wings. Not all insects have wings. Some, like the 2,000 different species of bloodsucking fleas, have lost them over the course of evolution. (Fleas, though, have developed something better for their particular lifestyle: back legs that let them jump enormous distances—a handy talent if you need to reach the underside of a dog or cat passing overhead.)

Insects were the first creatures to fly, and their wings are unique in the animal world. Unlike birds, bats, and the extinct pterosaurs (prehistoric reptiles that flew), insects did not have to give up a couple of limbs in exchange for wings. Their wings are actually outgrowths of their armored outer skin. They are formed of two extremely thin layers of chitin, with a network of delicate veins sandwiched between them. The veins fill with air or blood to stiffen the wings.

Most insects have four wings, one pair on the second segment of the thorax, and one on the third. But some—notably, flies and mosquitoes—have reduced that number to two. In place of their back pair, flies

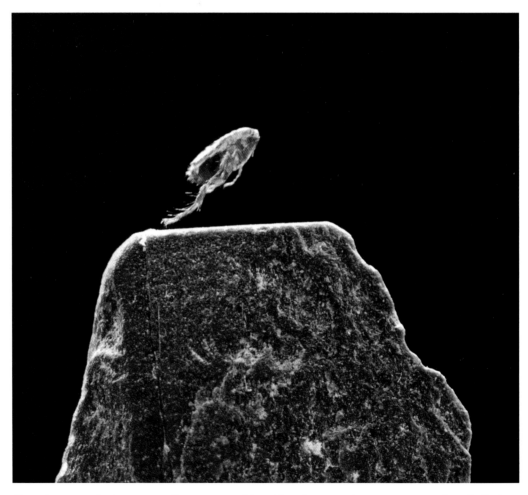

Fleas do not need wings—a cat flea can jump 10 to 12 inches to grab on to a passing furry belly. Its abilities come from a ball of springy protein squeezed down at the base of each leg.

have developed two club-shaped structures called halteres. The halteres stabilize and balance the insect during its acrobatic flight. In other insects, such as grasshoppers and beetles, the front wings have become hardened protective covers for the back wings, which are the only ones actually used in flying.

The most important difference between types of insect wings, though, is one that separates the "primitive" insects from the "advanced" insects. In the primitive group are the dragonflies and damselflies and mayflies, insects whose design dates back to the beginning of insect flight. These easily recognized fliers cannot fold their wings flat over their back. Dragonflies always have their wings stretched out, even when at rest. Damselflies always rest with wings upright.

Nearly all other winged insects are able to lay their wings back against their body. This ability was an important development in insect evolution. By tucking their wings out of the way, insects were able to crawl into tunnels and burrows, and into a lot of hiding, nesting, and feeding spaces that were not accessible to them before.

Dragonflies have a "primitive" arrangement of wings: they cannot fold back flat against the body.

Insects have evolved a great many variations on the basic theme of flying. For example, dragonflies differ from later fliers in that they beat their two pairs of wings independently. One pair goes up as the other goes down. This is possible because dragonflies have a separate set of muscles attached directly to each pair of wings. Later insects evolved ways to beat the two pairs together for more power and control. Butterflies, for example, use overlapping folds to join their front wings to their back wings. Bees and wasps have complicated hook-and-eye devices on the edges of their wings to make sure the two pairs flap as one.

How fast an insect beats its wings up and down depends a lot on how big it is. Generally, the smaller the insect, the more rapid the flapping. Some tiny flies actually beat their wings as fast as 1,000 times every second. Bigger bumblebees reach about 150 beats a second; mosquitoes, about 250. We can hear the difference as a change in pitch, from a low buzz to a high whine.

A moth's wings may look delicate, but they can carry the insect hundreds of miles.

The Abdomen

The third main section of the insect body, the abdomen, is made of a varying number of segments, but usually ten or eleven. The abdomen holds all the digestive organs, as well as the reproductive organs. The abdomen is more flexible than the other parts of the body. The segments can slide into one another like a set of stacking cups to allow the abdomen to stretch or shrink as necessary. In some insects, a change in abdominal size is needed to accommodate a large load of food. This is especially true for hardworking members of an ant colony that serve as "tanker trucks" filled with food for other ants in the nest. In some female insects, the abdomen must expand to hold a large cluster of eggs.

At the end of the abdomen, many insects have a pair of sensitive feelers, called cerci. Mostly these are used to keep insects aware of their surroundings, but some insects have turned their cerci into weapons. Earwigs, for instance, have a pair of curved, pointed cerci that they use to stab and grasp prey.

Some female insects also have at the end of the abdomen an organ called an ovipositor. This is a tool for inserting eggs into some desirable spot where the developing offspring will have sufficient

Many insects have sensitive "feelers," called cerci, on the tail end of their abdomen. Earwigs, though, have turned their cerci into weapons for stabbing prey.

Stingers on insects like honeybees are a female accessory. They evolved from ovipositors, body structures that females use to deposit their eggs in a suitable spot.

food or protection. The spot could be in soil, fruit, seeds, under the bark of a tree, or even deep inside the trunk. It could also be inside the body or eggs of another insect. Some ovipositors have sawtooth edges for cutting into wood, some have long hardened points. And some have also been turned into weapons. Bees and wasps have turned their pointed ovipositors into poisonous stingers, an evolutionary invention with which we humans are all too familiar.

CIRCULATION AND RESPIRATION

Unlike us, insects have no lungs for taking oxygen from the air and delivering it to the bloodstream. In fact, they do not have a bloodstream so much as a blood puddle, and it carries no oxygen.

Insects take air in directly through tiny holes, called spiracles, in the outside of their bodies. The spiracles lead to branching tubes called tracheae that carry the oxygen to all the tissues inside. Insect blood (which is called hemolymph), does perform tasks similar to those of our own blood. It brings nutrients from food to all the cells of the body, and it carries away wastes. Also, it is pumped by a heart. But the blood does not travel through a complex network of veins and arteries. Rather, it moves in a pool that sloshes through the entire inside of the body.

The insect's heart is really an elongated tube that runs from end to end along the insect's back, beneath the exoskeleton. Blood enters the tube through tiny holes at the rear. The heart then squeezes and pumps the blood forward, toward the head. There the blood exits the tube. Because the exoskeleton is rather rigid, the blood cannot really push out on the body and create bulging, blood-filled blisters. With nowhere else to go, the blood just naturally sloshes backward to bathe the insect's tissues.

Insects are ectothermic, or cold-blooded. Like reptiles, they have an internal temperature that goes up and down with the temperature of the air outside. Most cold-blooded creatures regulate their body temperatures by moving from warm areas to cooler ones, such as moving into the sunlight or into the shade. But insects have come up with a number of ways to get the heat they need. Butterflies, for example, use their wings while resting to gather up heat from sunlight. Large bumblebees and hawk moths get warm by shivering. The actions involved in shivering creates heat for the body. (For the most part, humans shiver for the same reason.)

DIGESTION

An insect's straightforward digestive system consists of a tube stretching from the mouth, where food goes in, to the anus, where waste goes out. The digestive tube is made of three parts, called the foregut, the midgut, and the hindgut.

From the mouth, food passes to a part of the foregut called the crop. There it is partially digested and sometimes stored for a while. From the crop the food moves into the gizzard, a part of the foregut that has especially muscular walls. By contracting and squeezing, the gizzard breaks down the food into even smaller bits. These pass into the midgut, the insect's stomach, where they are turned into liquid. Nutrients in this liquid flow through the stomach wall, into the blood, and off to other parts of the body. Whatever is left over flows into the hindgut, and the insect's intestine, and is eventually expelled through the anus.

Importantly, the digestive tube of many insects provides a home for bacteria and other microscopic creatures. Without them, insects would not be able to get any nourishment from some of the foods they eat. Termites, for example, cannot digest wood without an internal army of microscopic munchers helping them. Bloodsucking fleas and mosquitoes have their own tenants for help in digesting blood.

NERVOUS SYSTEM AND SENSES

An insect keeps its brain in its head—for the most part. The brain is in two sections. One receives information from the eyes and antennae, the other communicates with the mouthparts. From the brain two main nerve cords run through the bottom of the thorax and abdomen. Along the cords, in each segment, are clusters of nerve cells called ganglia that, to some degree, control activity in that segment. The brain acts as the central command center for the body, but the ganglia act as local command centers. Because of this arrangement, an insect's thorax or abdomen can generally continue to perform for a little while even if its head is missing.

Vision

To see, most insects have two large "compound" eyes made of many small lenses. Each lens is part of a single unit, or facet, that is usually hexagon-shaped (six-sided) and slightly curved. Fitted all together, the facets form a hemisphere. (Technically, each of these eye units is called an ommatidium.)

An insect's eye may have just a few facets or a huge number, depending on how big a role vision plays in the insect's life. Worker ants

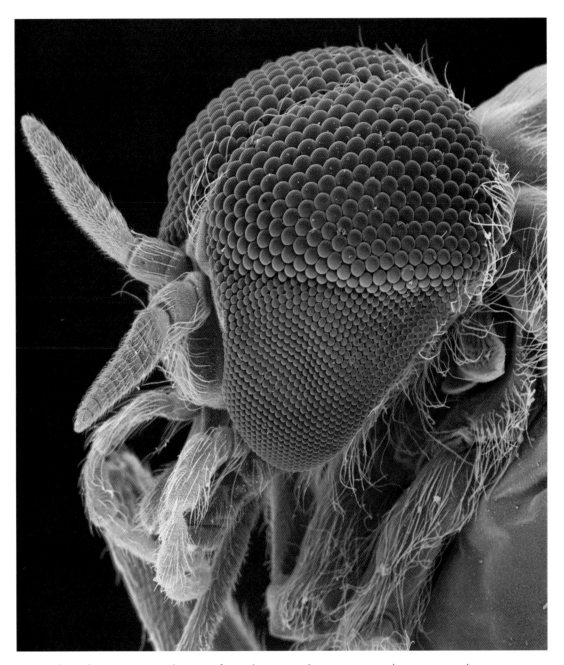

Seen through a microscope, the many-faceted compound eyes, segmented antennae, and sensitive hairs of a black fly make it look fearsome.

that spend all their time inside the nest have eyes made of six facets. Dragonflies, which range widely and are always on the lookout for food and predators, have as many as 30,000 facets in each eye.

It is difficult for us to imagine what an insect actually sees. Insect eyes do not move at all, and they can focus only within a shallow range—anything more than a few feet away is probably rather blurry. In addition, each facet is separate from the ones next to it, and each sees only a tiny portion of the scene in front of it. The result is that a dragonfly might see 30,000 separate, slightly overlapping pieces of the entomologist who is peering at it intently. The dragonfly must somehow put together all of these pieces.

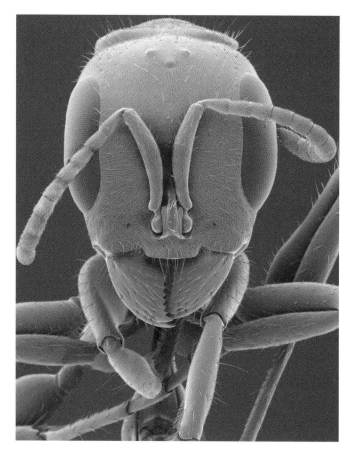

But most insects do not bother putting together whole images. They are much more geared toward noticing movement or changes in light than toward picking out fine details or shape. However, they can see a wider range of colors than we can. Our vision stops at the red and violet ends of the spectrum, but many insects can see

Along with their image-forming compound eyes, most insects have a triangle of three simple eyes, called ocelli, that detect only light and dark.

ultraviolet light and some can see infrared—abilities that we gain only with special "night-vision" and "heat-sensing" technology.

Along with their compound eyes, most insects also have three small simple eyes called ocelli. Often these are arranged in a triangle between the two larger eyes. Ocelli do not see images; they are more like sensors for light and dark. But they are important for seeking shade and hiding places, or for navigating by the light of the sun or moon. Many immature insects— some caterpillars, for instance—do not have any compound eyes, but they do have half a dozen ocelli on either side of their head.

Finally, some insects also have light-sensing cells dotting the length of their bodies. Among these are the night-loving, kitchen-stalking cockroaches that scatter at the flick of a distant bathroom light.

Hearing

Most insects do not have anything that we would recognize as ears. The major exceptions are, not surprisingly, the insects that make sounds for other insects to hear. Crickets usually have sound-sensitive membranes on their front legs, just below the "knee." Grasshoppers and cicadas hear with membranes on their abdomen.

But even some insects without ears detect sounds carried through the air. They hear through sound-sensitive hairs scattered across their body. Nocturnal insects—insects who are active in the night—have many of these hairs. Those same dark-loving roaches that sense the bathroom light with their bodies also hear footsteps with their tails—they have sound-sensing hairs lining their long rear-end feelers. Other insects have dense clusters of hairs covering their antennae. These hairs are tuned to vibrate in response to certain sounds. Male mosquitoes, for instance, hear the particular whine of a female mosquito's wings. (The male mosquitoes tend to respond differently than we humans do.)

In other insects these tiny hairs may respond to all sorts of stimulation: touch, humidity, air pressure, and even chemicals. The hairs on a housefly's antennae, for instance, are most sensitive to movement. They effectively warn the fly of any disturbance of the air around it—caused, for instance by the approach of a predator or a flyswatter.

Smell

Insects use other antennae hairs much as humans use their noses. Ground beetles find buried food through their antennae, and night-flying moths home in on a trail of nectar. Ants and bees use their antennae to smell and recognize members of their own colony.

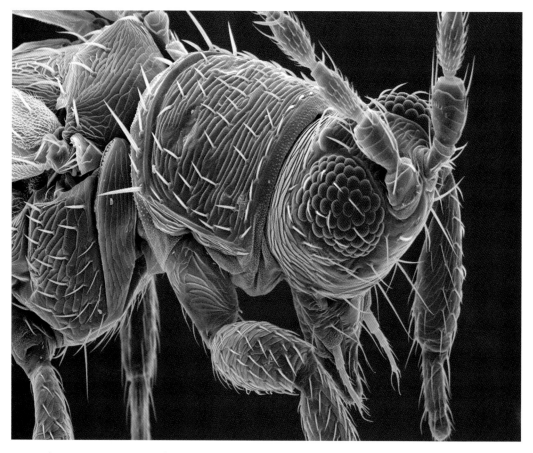

A tiny thrip grows to no more than .12 inch (3 mm). But it still comes fully equipped with all an insect's exquisitely designed parts. (Colors have been added to this photo to make structures more visible.)

The most important function of a moth's feathery antennae is to tune in the chemical signals, called pheromones, given off by a moth of the opposite sex. The insect shown here is a Polyphemus moth.

What those ants and bees are actually smelling are chemical signals called pheromones. Insects constantly use pheromones to communicate with one another. Often the messages are in the form of mating signals, sent from one sex to the other. Male moths, in particular, are experts at picking up the telltale pheromones wafted into the air by a female in search of a mate. A male silk moth can pick up the faint scent of pheromones released by a female three miles away.

Taste

Insects can taste things much as we do. They can distinguish sweet, sour, salty, and bitter tastes, and most even do so with the various parts of their mouth. But not always. Butterflies, along with moths, bees, and flies, also

Clean Machines

You may sometimes see a fly stop to clean all its sensors: eyes, antennae, feet, and body hairs. All are exquisitely adapted mechanisms that insects use for negotiating their way through a complicated world of other creatures. These sensors all must be kept spotless if they are to be useful. At the tiny scale of a fly, even a speck of dust can interfere with a foot's sensitive tastes.

Constant cleansing does not mean that flies are clean, though. Flies' mouthparts are like sponges that absorb liquid food. If a fly comes across something tasty that is not liquid, it basically spits on the food to liquefy it. Flies feed on a lot of things that we humans do not find especially appealing, such as garbage and manure. And these foods are often filled with bacteria. When a fly spits on kitchen food, it may be transferring millions of bacteria it picked up from its last meal. Those bacteria can cause a host of nasty diseases—for humans, that is, not for the thorough flies.

A fruit fly constantly cleans its legs to keep smell sensors on its feet from getting clogged.

This Eastern Black Swallowtail butterfly tastes the flower with its feet before it uses its proboscis to drink the flower's nectar.

use their feet—which is a highly efficient way of figuring out what is good to eat. If an insect can go rummaging with taste-sensing feet instead of a mouth, it can reserve its head for more important tasks, like watching for hungry predators. Besides, feet are likely to arrive at a food source first. This is why we often see flies walking along a countertop, then suddenly changing direction. The course change is not the result of a whim on the fly's part, or even the sight of a tasty morsel elsewhere. Rather, the fly is charting its course with its feet, following the tastiest trail.

Stinkbug nymphs do not differ drastically from stinkbug adults. They simply grow larger with each molt and continue to feed on the same food sources.

The Road to Maturity

To travel from birth to adulthood, an insect follows one of two main paths. They differ in how the insect spends its youth.

All insects start off as eggs. Once they hatch, the young insects begin to eat and grow, as do all animals. But before they reach full size, insects must go through a number of molts. The precise number varies with the species, from just a few to as many as thirty.

The way in which insects pass through the series of molts divides them into two groups. Basically, insects in the first group change a little as they grow. Insects in the second group change a lot. (To be entirely accurate, there is a third group, made up of the wingless, most primitive insects, such as the springtails and bristletails. These animals do not change at all as they age, except to get bigger with each molt.)

The key word in describing the division between the two is *metamorphosis*, which means a change in form or shape. The first group of insects undergoes gradual, or incomplete, metamorphosis. They have three stages in their development: egg, nymph, and adult. As immature nymphs, the young insects look more or less like smaller versions of adults, except that they have no wings. The wings appear only as "buds" that grow larger with each molt, along with the rest of the body. They finally appear in full form after the last molt, when the insect is an adult and able to reproduce. Nymphs also generally live in the same habitat as the adults and eat the same foods.

Insects belonging to the more ancient orders follow this path to adulthood. Cockroaches grow this way, as do grasshoppers, cicadas, crickets, katydids, termites, stick insects, termites, and mantises, among others. So do true bugs—-although nearly all of us use the name bug to describe any insect, to entomologists a bug is a particular kind of insect, one with mouthparts that both pierce and suck. Lots of true bugs boast of their status in their common names: bedbugs, stinkbugs, assassin bugs, leaf bugs, and water bugs, to name a few.

A green stinkbug lays its eggs on a leaf.

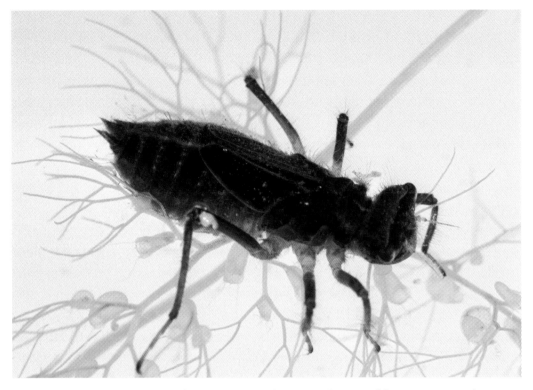

Unlike their adult versions, dragonfly nymphs live in the water. The powerful wings appear only as wing buds, but even without them the nymphs are mighty predators.

Dragonflies and damselflies and mayflies also undergo incomplete metamorphosis, but they lay their eggs in the water, and their nymphs lead aquatic lives, different from those of the adults. The nymphs of these insects are often called naiads.

Sometime before 270 million years ago and the first onstage appearance of the beetles, some insects developed a different pattern of growth. Their young looked very different from the adults, ate different foods, and often lived in different habitats. They also needed a fourth growth stage before adulthood. This was a resting stage, during which the young insects went through very dramatic changes before emerging as radically new creations. They went through complete metamorphosis.

The four developmental stages of these insects are called egg, larva, pupa, and adult. In general, the larvae (plural of *larva*) are wormlike creatures that may have no legs or many stumpy legs, no antennae, and often, no eyes. Caterpillars are a good example. They look so different from the adults that if we never saw one change into a moth we would never guess that they were both forms of the same animal. In fact, for very familiar insects, we give the larvae separate names: caterpillars, grubs (for beetle larvae), maggots (flies), wrigglers (mosquitoes).

In general, the larvae are eating machines, gorging themselves and growing larger until they are finally big enough to become adults. Then they stop eating completely. They may enclose themselves within a protective case or cocoon. At this stage tremendous events start to take place inside the cocoon. Nearly the entire body of the insect is broken down, then put back together again in a vastly different form. Segments are joined into the three divisions of head, thorax, and abdomen. Wings sprout. Compound eyes appear, along with reproductive organs. The fly, flea, wasp, bee, midge, mosquito, gnat, or ant that suddenly appears is so much more elaborate a creation than the one preceding it.

Complete metamorphosis offered participating insects a couple of distinct advantages. The first was that by having two forms as different as a caterpillar and a moth, the insect could live in at least two different habitats and feed on at least two different food sources (such as leaves and nectar). One effect of this arrangement was that no adult would have to complete with perhaps hundreds of youngsters for food.

The second advantage was that it allowed the insect to become a specialist at each stage of its life with a body custom designed for the task at hand. As a larva, an insect's job is to eat and grow; all it really needs is a mouth and a digestive tract. As an adult, its job is to mate and reproduce, so eyes, wings, and sensitive antennae become much more important. About 85 percent of insect species today follow this pattern of growth.

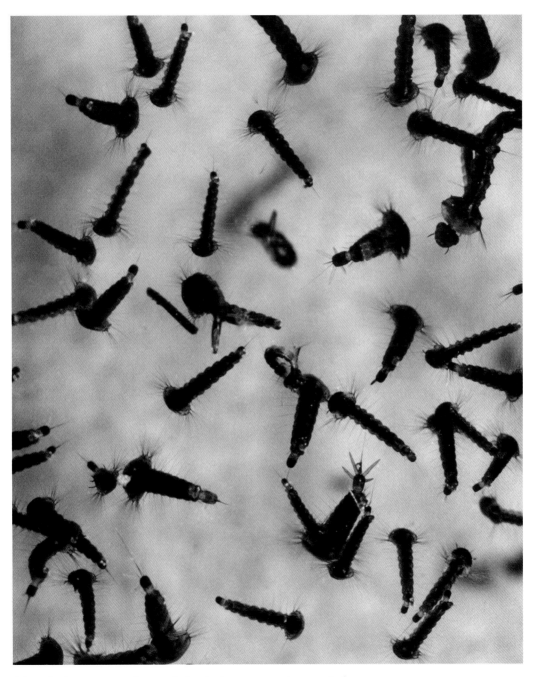

Mosquito larvae—sometimes called wrigglers—mature in a pool of water.

FINDING A MATE

No matter which pattern of growth they follow, all insect lives are aimed at the sole purpose of making more of their own kind. But short-lived adults cannot afford to waste much time finding a mate. To make sure they find the right member of the opposite sex quickly, they set all their sensors to maximum alert status.

In some species, sight plays a major mating role. Male butterflies, for example, are brilliantly colored to attract the notice of females. (Unfortunately, their color also attracts keen-eyed predators. Duller females live longer than the showy males.) The visual differences between the sexes may not always be so obvious to us. Luna moths, for example, all look pretty much alike to human eyes: large and pale green. But the wings of the male lunas reflect much more ultraviolet light than those of the female. The light is invisible to us, but to a female luna moth a male appears as a knight in ultraviolet-shining armor.

Other insects display differences in body form. Male stag beetles have huge, curved mandibles. These oversized jaws, much larger than a female's, are very similar to a deer's showy rack of antlers. Both animals use their adornments to impress females and fight with other males.

Visual appeal is carried to an extreme by lightning bugs, or fireflies. These members of the beetle family use their amazing ability to create a cold, bright light as a way to call out for interested mates. Generally, males fly around signaling to females, who have climbed up on a bush or a tall blade of grass to watch the show. Different firefly species distinguish themselves both by the color of their light—it ranges from pale red to yellow-green—and the code of their flashes. Distinctions are important, since there are about 2,000 firefly species. So each male uses its species' particular sequence of on and off to search for a proper companion in the darkness.

But for fireflies, as for humans, codes are made to be broken. Females of the firefly genus Photuris have learned to mimic the flash

Male stag beetles sport "horns" for the same reason male deer grow antlers: to fight with other males and win mates. The beetle's horns are actually enlarged jaws.

sequences of many species besides their own. A male, seeing a glowing response to his flashy advertising, will zoom in to land next to what he no doubt thinks is the light of his life. Sadly for him, the *Photuris* female has called him over not for mating but only for dinner—her dinner.

Other familiar insects span the distance between them by sound. For more than 300 million years crickets, cicadas, katydids, and grasshoppers have been singing their songs of love and longing, and they have been doing it without the aid of voices. Insects have no vocal cords. They make sound by vibrating other parts of their body.

Some grasshoppers sing by rubbing the upper part of their rear legs against the underside of their wings, which they have folded back. Legs and wings both are lined with ridges or small pegs, so that rubbing one against the other is like running a fingernail against a comb or a washboard. Other grasshoppers, and all crickets, scrape the bottom of one forewing over the top of the other.

Cicadas go in for a different manner of noisemaking. They have a membrane in their abdomen that works like the skin of a drum. Muscles in the abdomen make the membrane flex up and down. Each time it bends, it makes a clicking noise. Enough of these clicks put together—and cicadas can flex that membrane nearly 400 times a second—makes for an earsplitting whine, at least to our ears. To a cicada, apparently, it is heavenly music.

We can easily see the flashes of fireflies and hear the songs of crickets, but other messages sent between insects escape our notice completely. Pheromones fall into this category, of course. So do some extraordinarily subtle vibrations.

Delicate water striders, for instance, move over the surface of a pond or stream by using the surface "skin" of the water and their water-repellant feet to hold them up. But they also use the surface of the water to send messages. By gently tapping with their legs, male striders send signals to females. The vibrations, carried in faint ripples on the surface, are in code, like the flashes of fireflies.

Treehoppers, also known as thornbugs, spend most of their lives sitting on stems of plants, sucking out the sap. Chiefly they avoid predators by their appearance, which is that of a sharp pointed thorn, and do not like to move unnecessarily. When it is time to mate, male thorn bugs search for females by vibrating their abdomen against the stem of the plant. The sound is carried through the stem, and any resident female will respond with a vibration of her own.

REPRODUCTION

After finding a mate and mating, a female insect lays her eggs. The number of eggs varies widely with the species. Some lay only a few dozen, some a few thousand, and some hundreds of millions. Termite queens may lay more than 10,000 eggs a day.

Those termite eggs will receive a lot of care from the army of workers within the nest. So will the eggs of other social insects, such as bees and ants, and even of a few non-social insects, such as roaches and earwigs. Most insects, however, do little to protect their eggs or their hatched

Termites tend to their queen as she lays eggs. Termite queens are several times larger than regular termites. Their larger size allows them to lay thousands of eggs each day.

Average Insect life spans

Bee queen	6 years
worker	6 months
drone	8 weeks
One-hour midge	30 minutes (as adult)
Mayfly	24 hours (as adult)
Housefly	males: 27 days
	females: 37 days
Cicada	17 years in northern regions
	13 years in southern regions
Fruitfly	21 days
Bed bug	4 months (as adult)
Love bug	2 days (as adult)
No-see-um	2 years
American cockroach	1 year

offspring. A mayfly, which as an adult lives for only several hours, may lay 3,000 eggs. But she will just drop them onto the surface of a stream or lake where most will certainly be eaten. Many insects follow this pattern—they depend on the large number of eggs they produce to make sure that at least a couple survive.

For most insects, life as an adult is brief. The cicada, for instance, spends nearly all of its seventeen years as a nymph, living underground, and only a few months as an adult above ground. Many other adult insects survive only a few weeks, and some only hours. Tiny one-hour midges live even less than their name suggests—only 30 minutes, on average.

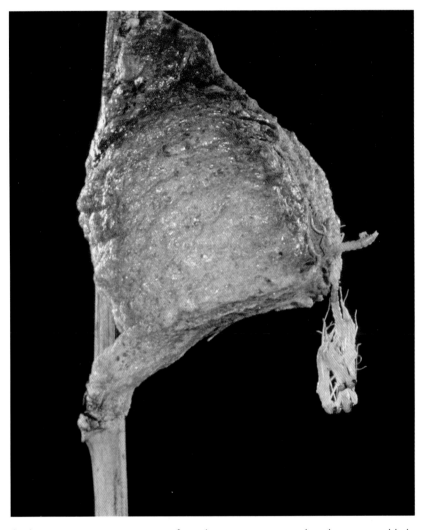

Newly hatched praying mantises, emerging from their egg case, are already recognizable by their body structure. Mantises do not go through complete metamorphosis.

There are exceptions to this rule, found among the social insects. In their complex societies, a single, well-tended egg-laying ant queen can survive for thirty years or more. A termite queen may survive even longer—for as much as fifty years according to some reports.

Insect Homes

Most adult insects do not need to build homes for themselves. For protection against predators or weather, they rely on whatever handy nook or crevice they can find. But for immature insects, shelter is often necessary.

A number of insects make their homes in or on plants. The larvae of froghoppers, or "spittlebugs," create a frothy mound around themselves by secreting fluid from glands in their abdomen, then whipping it up with air. Their foamy home protects them as they suck on plant juices. Certain wasps take a more aggressive approach. They inject a substance into a plant stem that forces the stem to swell into a lump called a gall. Eggs laid within the stem hatch into wasp larvae that find themselves enclosed in a sturdy shelter that keeps them both safe and well fed.

Other wasps build clusters of tube shaped nests out of mud and saliva. Some solitary bees (bees that do not live in large colonies) make similar nests, or fashion cigar-shaped cells from snipped off pieces of leaves.

But the real champions of insect homebuilders are the social bees, ants, and termites. The hive of a honeybee is a marvel of engineering that offers a secure, well-stocked nursery for the queen bee's legions of offspring. The maze-like networks of tunnels and chambers that make up many different anthills are equally impressive. The largest anthills may be palaces that shelter as many as 500,000 individual residents.

Termites put even the mighty ants to shame. Mound-building termites in Africa and Australia build towering homes that may rise 10 to 16 feet (3 to 5 m) in the air. Made of dirt and minerals and saliva, the walls of the mound are rock hard and give the colony maximum protection. Inside, a labyrinth of air tunnels ventilates the massive home and keeps it from overheating.

African termite mounds are some of the most elaborate insect homes on Earth.

Ladybugs are not dainty diners. To the delight of farmers and gardeners, these ferocious beetles eat huge numbers of plant-sucking aphids.

Eating Well, Living Dangerously

Insects owe much of their tremendous evolutionary success to two characteristics: their small size, and their ability to adapt, or to change in response to changing conditions in the world around them. These immensely valuable qualities have allowed them to spread across the globe and to survive even as other animals disappeared in great waves of extinction. They have also allowed insects to squeeze into every possible nook in, on, above, and below Earth's surface. With the general (though not quite complete) exception of the oceans, insects have found a way to live anywhere in the world. Larvae of insects called brine flies have even been found living in pools of crude oil, and in water as salty as the Dead Sea. Others have been found in hot springs, in temperatures of 120 degrees Fahrenheit (49 degrees C).

Insects live anywhere they can find food, and they eat a lot of different foods, from paper to pepper and from dead bodies to dung. But, in general, insects can be grouped as plant-eaters or meat-eaters or eaters of everything. Within each of these groups we can make further distinctions. We can separate those insects that chew plants, for instance, from those that sip nectar. Or we can separate insects that hunt live animals from those that scavenge the bodies of dead ones. But we must keep in mind that many insects belong to more than one group, since they follow one diet during their immature stage and another during their adult stage.

THE PLANT-EATERS

Most insects live off plants at some stage of their life. Some eat leaves, others suck sap. Still others focus on fruit, seeds, or roots. All have mouths shaped and suited for their favored foods.

The hungriest leaf chewers seem to be caterpillars. The luna moth caterpillar, for example, which weighs about two-thousandths of an ounce (.05 gram) to start, eats roughly 120 leaves and increases its weight some

Like all caterpillars, the zebra butterfly larva has only one goal: to eat as much as possible. To keep undisturbed by other eaters, its body is filled with toxins.

66

4,000 times before its stops eating and wraps itself in a plus-size cocoon. Some caterpillars grow large enough that they can easily be heard chomping away. Others are so small that they fit inside the leaf, chewing tunnels between the leaf's top and bottom surfaces. Some fly and beetle larvae also tunnel this way.

Among the great sap suckers are the aphids, which drive many human gardeners crazy. The aphids greedily drink up all the plant juice they can, killing the prized plants as they go. Other suckers include bugs that like to live only on the sap of grapevines.

Many insects dine on seeds, among them various species of chewing ants and beetles. Roots are attacked by both chewers and suckers. In the first group are the larvae of beetles that live underground. Among the suckers are the nymphs of cicadas, which live underground also, and for many years. Part of the reason the nymphs take so long to develop may be that they do not get all that much nutrition from their tough food. With a poor diet, they grow and mature slowly.

Finally, there are a very large number of insects that feed on nectar from flowering plants. Bees, flies, butterflies, moths, mosquitoes, and many, many more families of insects find sugary nectar an especially desirable, energy-rich food. Many also eat the pollen. A variety of bees, in fact, depend on pollen as food for their larvae. They carry it back to the hive in special containers on their hind legs, called pollen baskets.

THE MEAT-EATERS

Meat-eaters, on the other hand, are a minority among insects. But they are a highly visible and effective minority. They are also insects we depend on. Without them, the plant-eating insects would be unstoppable, and our lives would be greatly affected.

Like plant-eaters, meat-eaters also can be described as chewers or suckers, each with their specialized mouthparts. But we can also group them by their method of attack. There are the active hunters, the stealthy ambushers, the parasites, and the carrion eaters. What they all have in common is that, one way or another, they get their nutrition from the bodies of other animals. They are all also considerably more dramatic than plant-eaters.

We need only to look at the ancient dragonfly to realize how long and how efficiently insects have been eating their own kind. The dragonflies' method of hunting has probably changed very little over the hundreds of millions of years that they have been on Earth, though their food has. Many of the species they dine on today did not exist when the first dragonflies started patrolling the skies. But like most insect hunters, dragonflies are flexible. With their large eyes, powerful wings, and strong jaws, a dragonfly will hunt down almost any right-sized thing that flies.

The dragonfly's technique is to snatch something out of the air with its front legs, then bring it up to its mouth. Usually it eats while flying, tossing aside any body parts that it does not want. It is noticeably a chewer and a cruncher.

Other chewing hunters prowl the ground. Some are very fast. Tiger beetles, for example, equipped with large sickle-shaped jaws, can race after and overtake their prey much as a big cat can. An Australian tiger beetle, incidentally, holds the current record for the world's fastest insect runner. It has been clocked at 8.2 feet per second (2.5 mps), which for this insect means that in every second it is running 120 times the length of its .8-inch (2 cm) body. To match that, a six-foot human would have to run at a speed of 491 miles per hour (790 kmh).

Not all hunters need to be fast, however. Ladybugs, for instance, have a tremendous appetite for plant-sucking aphids and hunt down herds of them daily. But the aphids are so sluggish that a ladybug can simply amble along at the speed of a slow vacuum cleaner.

Some of the insect world's most interesting hunters are water dwellers. Backswimmers are predators that swim upside-down just below the surface of freshwater ponds and lakes. They feed on nearly everything they can find, from other insects to tiny fish and tadpoles. Their method of attack is to grab prey with their front and middle legs (their long, fringed hind legs are their oars). Then they stab the catch with their pointy "beak" and inject it with digestive juices. Backswimmers are true bugs, and they take no solid food. They must turn their food into liquid before they can suck it into their mouths.

Some predators prefer their insect food to come to them rather than the other way around. Generally, of course, other insects prefer not to be eaten, so the would-be ambusher needs a winning technique. One strategy is the "hide in plain sight" approach. The praying mantis provides the most spectacular example. Mantises are usually colored brown or green to blend in with the plants on which they sit. (An Asian species, though, is pink to match the flowers it hangs out on.) All are quite good at keeping perfectly still for as long as it takes until food—in the form of a fly, a butterfly, or even a wasp or a bee—comes within reach of its overdeveloped grasping front legs. When it does, the mantis moves, and moves fast. It can reach out so fast, that should it miss on its first grab at a fly, it can make a second attempt before the fly has had time to take off.

A second ambushing technique calls for true hiding. The antlion is a notable practitioner of this craft. Antlions are predators as larvae, and they start laying their traps as soon as they leave the egg. The trap is a pit that the antlion digs in sandy soil by walking backward in a circle, and tossing out shovelfuls of sand with its head. Once the pit is deep enough, the antlion half-buries itself at the bottom, its huge curved jaws held open, and waits for an ant to blunder over the edge. When it does, the ant is likely to lose its footing on the slippery slope—some antlions help by tossing sand at it—and come tumbling down into the open mouth of the hunter at the bottom of the pit.

Finally, there are ambushers who go in for the "sheep in wolf's clothing"' technique. Among these are the aptly named assassin bugs. One type disguises itself by wearing the skin of a past meal. The assassin bug pulls the uneaten exoskeleton of a termite onto its back, then wanders

A praying mantis relies on both its ability to sit absolutely still and its lightning-fast reflexes once prey comes within reach of its powerful front legs.

The antlion has perfected the art of ambush. It digs a small crater in loose soil, then buries itself and waits for an ant to come sliding down the slippery walls of its trap.

straight into the termite's nest. Unchallenged, it quickly snares another meal, and another disguise.

Some predators seek meat not for themselves but for their offspring. Some of the most notorious members of this group are parasitic wasps. Their techniques vary, but the basic aim of them all is to subdue prey by stinging it and then using the body as food for developing eggs or larvae. Sometimes this involves laying the eggs inside the prey animal—often a spider or a caterpillar—so the hatched larvae can eat the still-living animal from the inside out. Other wasps paralyze their prey, then bury it alive with their larvae.

Wasps of this type belong to a number of species, come in a great variety of sizes, and show preferences for an equal variety of victims. Some are large enough to specialize in tarantulas. Some are so tiny that they can lay their eggs inside the eggs of other insects.

Included among the animal feeders, though they are of a different sort, are the bloodsucking insects. We are painfully familiar with the ones that have a taste for human blood—fleas, lice, bedbugs, biting flies, mosquitoes. But many others exist, dining on other animals of every description.

All bloodsuckers have mouths specifically designed for the task, with parts that pierce the skin and other parts that act like straws. The mosquito's mouth is one of the most elegant. Its many mouthparts have evolved into six sharp needlelike instruments, called stylets, that are all held within a larger protective tube formed from the labium (the lower lip). Four of the stylets are for piercing the skin; the other two are squeezed together to form a groove through which the blood is sucked.

Only female mosquitoes dine on humans—they need the blood to nourish their eggs. Males are nectar feeders. The same is not true of the other insects that routinely pierce human skin. Fleas of both sexes, in fact, must have a blood meal before they will get together to mate.

THE SCAVENGERS

Finally, there are insects that make their living off the dead. These insects are sometimes thought of as Earth's housekeepers. They keep the planet from being filled with litter. Some of these are actually plant-eaters, or at least dead-plant-eaters. A variety of small insects, among them the tiny, primitive springtails and bristletails, turn dead leaves into soil and recycle nutrients that would otherwise be lost.

Another contingent of insects works on dead animals, quickly eating the flesh of anything that does not move. Chief among these are blowflies and burying beetles. The flies do not actually eat the dead meat,

Dung beetles roll up balls of animal waste to feed their young. To ancient Egyptians, these beetles were reminiscent of the god Ra rolling the sun across the sky.

they lay their eggs in it, and the maggots do the eating. The beetles both eat the meat themselves and store it for their larvae.

Other beetles specialize in eating animal dung, which may strike us as repulsive. But dung is high in nutrition, since it consists of only partly digested food. For dung beetles, it is a treasure. Different species around the world feast on the droppings of large mammals from cattle to camels to elephants to humans. Typically, the beetles roll the dung into a ball and bury it, both to store it as a future food source for their young and to get it out of sight of other greedy dung grabbers. Dung apparently makes for strong chitin and healthy bodies. Among the dung beetles is the world's heaviest insect, the 6-inch (15.2 cm), quarter-pound (113.4 g) African Goliath beetle.

A hawk moth caterpillar in the Costa Rican rain forest adopts a convincing disguise to avoid being eaten. When disturbed, it inflates its head to look like a poisonous snake.

Surviving, for Better and Worse

Nearly all insects are hunted as food, and not just by other insects. Birds, mammals, lizards, snakes, frogs, toads, and especially spiders all depend on insect meals for their survival.

Insects, naturally, have developed a few ways to avoid joining any of these companions for dinner. Their principle response to attack is to try to escape. No matter how well-armed or -legged an insect might be, it is always far better to flee than to fight. The need to escape predators was surely at least one of the pressures behind the development of insect wings. Wings enable insects to accomplish several other important tasks, of course, such as finding food, mates, and new territory. But their value as an escape tool is very high.

Certain insect bodies have developed other specialized parts for escaping a hungry predator's claws and jaws. These include jumping legs in froghoppers, for example, or "ears" in certain night-flying moths that can hear the echolocating calls of bats. (Echolocation is the sound-wave process some animals use to identify and locate objects.) More generalized

Many insects, like this katydid, have evolved spiky growths of chitin that make them undesirable food for animals without teeth, such as birds.

features include the flattened body of roaches and bugs that allow them to squeeze into impossibly narrow hiding places.

CHEMICAL WEAPONRY

A large variety of insects try to avoid predators by making themselves extremely unpleasant to eat. Most children have learned that grasshoppers, for instance, spit "tobacco juice" when threatened. The juice is actually the partly digested food from the insect's crop, and it is not so much spit as vomited. It is as unappealing to some predators as it sounds (though not to all—some predators have no taste). Other insects have similar defenses. Stinkbugs, for example, simply stink. Certain water beetles fire pellets of waste from their rear ends as they swim away from pursuing fish.

These are all mild forms of chemical warfare. Bombardier beetles go in for a more serious version. These insects get their name from their ability to "bomb" an attacker with a series of gas explosions from their abdomen. A mixture of chemicals inside their body results in the emission of a hot, brownish spray that can burn any predator that gets too near. Other beetles ooze out peppery liquids, some from their legs, others from glands inside their forewings. These substances are often powerful enough to burn human skin.

Many insects make sure they are not just bad tasting but poisonous. Monarch butterflies, when caterpillars, gorge themselves on the leaves of milkweed plants. A chemical in the leaves guarantees that a predator foolish enough to eat a monarch caterpillar will soon vomit up its meal. If it does not, it will die. Adult butterflies continue to carry the milkweed poison they ate as youngsters.

Of course, this method of defense does little for the butterfly that has already been eaten. By the time the predator learns its

When threatened, a bombardier beetle mixes an array of chemicals in a chamber in its abdomen. Combined, the chemicals explode out in a hot spray that sends predators running.

lesson, the butterfly is history. But it does protect other butterflies in the future. And poisonous insects usually try to get their message across before being eaten. Most of them are brightly colored or marked with bold black-bordered stripes.

MIMICRY AND CAMOUFLAGE

The monarch's poison defense is so effective that another butterfly, the viceroy, uses it also. Unlike the monarch, though, the viceroy cannot eat milkweed. In fact, any predator can munch on a viceroy with no ill effects whatsoever—no vomiting, no dying. However, the viceroy has evolved so

A drone fly wears the yellow and black markings of a stinging wasp or bee, but it is all for show—the fly actually has no stinger.

A thornbug goes in for a double defense: it both looks and feels as distasteful as a thorn. To complete the deception, the bug rarely moves.

that it sports the same orange wings with black lines and white spots that adorn the monarch. Birds that have learned to avoid the poisonous monarch will avoid the non-poisonous viceroy as well.

This kind of defense is called mimicry, and it is not limited to butterflies. Stinging insects, for example, like bees, are often marked by black and yellow stripes that predators quickly grow wary of. The drone fly has taken advantage of this by evolving a striped body similar to that of a bee. Many predators, seeing the drone fly's black and yellow outfit, simply let it pass. In fact the drone fly is harmless, its weaponry non-existent.

Other insects try not so much to look like something else as to look like nothing at all. They camouflage themselves so that they fade into the background. Stick insects blend in among twigs and bark. Treehoppers look, and often feel, like thorns. Leaf butterflies look convincingly like dead leaves. Some caterpillars look like bird droppings.

Most insect lives are governed by the basic rules of predators and prey: eat what you can while avoiding being eaten by others. But not all insect relationships are antagonistic. Some are symbiotic—cooperative arrangements with other organisms that work out to the benefit of both sides.

The most common example is the relationship between insects and flowering plants. In exchange for food, insects carry pollen from flower to flower and help the plants reproduce. But some insects have established more complicated relationships with plants. In South America, certain species of ants live inside the hollow thorns of acacia trees. There they feed on nectar and tiny fruits that grow at the base of the leaves. In return, the ants lend the plant the benefit of their strong jaws and stingers to repel other, leaf-eating ants. They also keep the area around the tree free of nutrient-grabbing weeds.

Ants figure in a number of the symbiotic relationships found in the insect world. Several species of ants grow mushroom-like fungi in their nests, which they use as food. The fungus benefits by being fully protected and nurtured. It is in the ants' interest, after all, to make sure that their fungus crop thrives and reproduces.

Other ants raise herds of aphids or scale insects. These smaller creatures normally suck the sugary liquids out of plant stems and leaves. The aphids excrete, or get rid of, any excess sugar in the form of tiny droplets called honeydew. Honeydew, for ants, is an energy-packed food. It is well worth their time to protect the aphids as they feed in exchange for the honeydew they produce. Some ants even take the aphids into their nests.

In Europe, some ants milk the honeydew-producing caterpillars of the blue butterfly. The ants search out the caterpillars, carry them underground, and keep them fed while they grow. When it is time for the caterpillar to pupate, the ants carry it back outside.

Other insects form partnerships with much larger animals. Some beetles, for example, live on rodents such as mice and shrews. They cling to the animal's fur, just like a bloodsucking insect, but they have no interest in the rodent itself. Instead they feed on the real blood-suckers—fleas and lice—that often torment the furry mammal. Naturally, the rodents are happy to give the beetles a warm home and free transportation.

Finally, many termites and wood-boring beetles would starve to death were it not for the services of tiny protoctists that live in their digestive tract. Without them, the insects would never be able to digest the cellulose in the wood they eat so greedily.

Many ant species farm herds of aphids, which they "milk" for the sweet liquid honeydew the aphids produce. In return the aphids get the ants' protection.

No matter what defense an insect relies on, the brutal truth is that very few of them will die of old age. Insects are a vast food source for animals of every kind, including the insects themselves. In addition, despite the exquisite design of the insect body, it is still a small fragile thing when compared with the physical forces of weather. Insects can avoid some of the effects of nature. Most can go into a resting, or hibernating, state as an egg or larva or even as an adult. Ladybugs in California, for example, gather in huge colonies to hibernate in the mountains in winter, then return to the valleys in the spring. While they are resting, each ladybug releases a small amount of a predator-repelling substance. The total volume of it protects them all. Other insects migrate to avoid the cold. Monarch butterflies escape winter by flying south—sometimes as much as 2,000 miles (3,200 km) from Canada to Mexico.

Still, the weather takes its toll, and what the elements do not kill, the predators will. Only a relatively few insect eggs ever hatch. Few of those that do ever make it to adulthood. The odds against an insect egg developing into an insect parent are very, very high. Of course, insects lay a staggering number of eggs. And the world is still populated by a staggering number of insects.

INSECTS v. HUMANS?

The insects' dependence on numbers is what so often makes them a problem for us. Huge congregations of them eat huge amounts of food. Any crop-eating insect, in large enough numbers, can be a serious threat to a human food supply. Marauding swarms of locusts, for example, are modern as well as Biblical plagues. Blanketing fields by the millions, they utterly destroy the food supplies of entire nations. We are constantly battling such pests as flies that eat our fruit or wheat, chinch bugs that devour our corn, cotton-eating boll weevils, and potato-ravaging beetles, to name just a few. Meanwhile, silverfish eat our books and clothing, termites destroy our homes, and cockroaches raid our kitchens.

This swarm of locusts devastated crops in the Philippines in 1994. In 2004, just as in biblical times, locusts plowed through North Africa and the Mideast.

Then there are the insects that kill us directly. Flies, fleas, and mosquitoes all carry diseases that have wreaked havoc on human populations for centuries. They have killed untold millions of people with bubonic plague, malaria, yellow fever, sleeping sickness, typhus, dengue fever, encephalitis, Chagas' disease, and more. In doing so they have shaped human history: plague-carrying fleas virtually emptied medieval Europe; tsetse flies and sleeping sickness kept a huge chunk of Africa off-limits to farmers and cows; mosquitoes have brought fever and death to millions of people especially in tropical regions. Mosquito-transmitted malaria still kills more than 2 million people every year. Other mosquito-borne infections, such as West Nile virus, are a growing threat.

Yet, for all the pain and suffering a relatively few insects bring us, we could hardly wish to be rid of them all. Most importantly, we depend on them for pollinating the plants that we eat. Were there no insects to do the job, we would literally starve to death. Also important are the products we get directly from insects, such as honey and silk.

We are far more dependent on insects than most of us realize. They are critical to our lives, from the most sophisticated levels of scientific research to the most basic levels of existence. For example, much of what we know about how our genes work in fashioning our bodies, we have learned from studying the genes of the tiny fruit fly. Although a fruit fly is vastly different from a human, all the way up to the level of phylum, its DNA and its genes are remarkably similar. Scientists breed and use fruit flies to learn about heredity and genetics.

A more basic dependence on insects is not as obvious, but it is no less real. In many parts of the world, insects have been an important food source for humans, as they are for other animals. Beetle larvae, ants, and grasshoppers have all provided people with needed protein for centuries.

We have a still deeper dependence on the scavenging insects. Although we do not like to think about them, we need them to break down and recycle animal wastes and dead plants and bodies of all sizes and shape. In any forest, or on any damp patch of ground anywhere in the world, armies of tiny springtails and bristletails are breaking down leaf litter. Across the globe, a variety of flies and beetles are picking apart dead flesh and dung and returning their nutrients to the earth. If, by some unimaginable catastrophe, these ancient recyclers were all to perish, we would, too. Without them soil everywhere would quickly become too poor to support large plants. Plant-eating animals would die, and with them, all other animals also.

In the end, we are so thoroughly intertwined with the members of the class Insecta that we cannot possibly do without them. Would insects, if they could think, ever think the same of us? Probably not. A few insects—certain mosquitoes and fleas—might be affected. But if we humans were suddenly gone, most insects would either not notice our departure or quickly adapt to the changed world. They would find foods

Some insects we find repellant, while others we see as beautiful. But without all of them, our world would be utterly unlivable.

other than our crops to eat, places other than our farms and homes to live in. They would simply go on doing precisely what they have been doing since life on the land began, dominating the planet with their variety and their great numbers and not worrying whether some future intelligent observer will ever arrive to make sense of them all.

G L O S S A R Y

abdomen—The rear section of an insect's three main body divisions.

arthropod—A member of the phylum Arthropoda, the largest group of animals on Earth; all of which have jointed legs and a body divided into segments. The class Insecta forms the biggest arthropod group.

chitin—The hard material that forms an insect's exoskeleton.

crop—Section of the digestive tube where food is first partially digested and sometimes stored.

exoskeleton—The toughened outer skin of an arthropod, which protects and provides support for the body.

ganglion—A cluster of nerve cells.

gizzard—Muscular section of the digestive tube where food is ground and crushed.

labium—One of the insect's mouthparts, the lower "lip."

labrum—Another mouthpart, the upper "lip."

larva—An immature stage of an insect that undergoes complete metamorphosis.

mandibles—The two primary jaws of an insect.

maxillae—The insect's secondary, or assistant, pair of jaws.

metamorphosis—A change in body form as the insect reaches maturity.

mimicry—The physical imitation of one animal by another; for example, of a poisonous insect by one that is harmless.

molt—The shedding of the exoskeleton.

naiad—An immature dragonfly or damselfly.

nymph—The immature stage of an insect that undergoes incomplete metamorphosis.

ocelli—Small, simple eyes, used for detecting light and dark.

ommatidium—A single unit, or facet, of the insect's compound eye.

organism—An individual living thing; a single plant or animal.

palps—Fingerlike mouthparts used for manipulating and tasting food.

pheromone—A chemical scent often used by male and female animals to attract each other.

protoctist—A member of the kingdom Protoctista, distinct from the bacteria, and most often a single-celled or microscopic organism.

pupa—The final immature stage of an insect that undergoes complete metamorphosis.

species—The basic unit of classification that defines a "specific" type of animal or plant; to date, there are roughly 1,000,000 insect species identified.

spiracle—An opening in the surface of the body that leads to one of the tracheae, the tubes that supply air to the insect's.

taxonomy—The science of biological classification.

thorax—The middle of the three sections of the insect's body, to which the legs and wings are attached.

tracheae—The air-carrying tubes inside the insect's body.

INSECT

CLASS INSECTA
several dozen orders; can be
grouped by type of metamorphosis

PRIMITIVE, WINGLESS INSECTS, WITH NO METAMORPHOSIS

Collembola (springtails)
Diplura (two-pronged bristletails)
Protura (proturans)
Thysanura (three-tailed bristletails
   and silverfish)

INSECTS WITH INCOMPLETE METAMORPHOSIS

Ephemeroptera (mayflies)
Odonata (dragonflies and damselflies)
Blattodea (cockroaches)
Dermaptera (earwigs)
Embioptera (web-spinners)
Isoptera (termites)
Mantodea (praying mantises)
Orthoptera (crickets, grasshoppers,
   katydids, locusts)
Phasmatodea (stick insects)
Plecoptera (stoneflies)
Grylloblattodea (rockcrawlers)
Mantophasmatodea (gladiators)
Hemiptera (true bugs):
   suborder Homoptera (leafhoppers,
      cicadas, aphids, scale insects,
      whiteflies)
   suborder Heteroptera (true bugs)
Phthiraptera (lice):
   Mallophaga (biting lice)
   Anoplura (sucking lice)
Psocoptera (book and bark lice)
Thysanoptera (thrips)
Zoraptera (zorapterans)

FAMILY TREE

INSECTS WITH COMPLETE METAMORPHOSIS

Coleoptera (beetles)
Diptera (true flies, gnats, midges, mosquitoes)
Hymenoptera (sawflies, wasps, hornets, ichneumons, ants, bees)
Lepidoptera (moths and butterflies)
Mecoptera (scorpionflies)
Neuroptera (lacewings and antlions)
Megaloptera (alder flies)
Raphidioptera (snake flies)
Siphonaptera (fleas)
Strepsiptera (stylopids—tiny, uncommon "twisted wing" parasites)
Trichoptera (caddisflies, sedge flies)

F U R T H E R   R E A D I N G

Berenbaum, May R. *Ninety-nine Gnats, Nits, and Nibblers.* Urbana: University of Illinois Press, 1989.

————. *Ninety-nine More Maggots, Mites, and Munchers.* Urbana: University of Illinois Press, 1993

Conniff, Richard. *Spineless Wonders: Strange Tales from the Invertebrate World.* New York: Henry Holt and Company, Inc., 1996.

Fleisher, Paul. *AnimalWays: Ants.* NY: Marshall Cavendish Benchmark, 2002.

Hostetler, Mark. *That Gunk on Your Car: A Unique Guide to Insects of the United States.* Gainesville, Fla.: Brazen Cockroaches, Inc., 1997.

Kneidel, Sally. *Stink Bugs, Stick Insects, and Stag Beetles: And 18 More of the Strangest Insects on Earth.* New York: John Wiley and Sons, 2000.

Nuridsany, Claude and Marie Pérennou. *Microcosmos: The Invisible World of Insects.* New York: Stewart, Tabori & Chang, 1997.

Menzel, Peter and Faith D'Aluisio. *Man Eating Bugs: The Art and Science of Eating Insects.* Berkeley, Cal.: Ten Speed Press, 1990.

O'Toole, Christopher. *Alien Empire.* New York: HarperCollins, 1995.

Schwabacher, Martin. *AnimalWays: Bees.* New York: Marshall Cavendish Benchmark, 2003.

http://www.pbs.org/wnet/nature/alienempire/

Alien Empire, the Web companion to the PBS Nature miniseries on insects, has photos, graphics and games.

http://bohart.ucdavis.edu/kidscorner.asp

The Bohart Museum of Entomology at the University of California at Davis has a dedicated "Kids corner" with great information and images.

http://ufbir.ifas.ufl.edu/

The University of Florida Book of Insect Records posts the most up-to-date information on insect record holders. It has fantastic information, and is a great way to understand the applications of the scientific method.

http://www.bugbios.com/index.html

Bugbios, a site with many photos meant to fascinate all ages.

The author found these sources especially helpful when researching this book.

Cocroft, Rex. "Thornbug to Thornbug." *Natural History,* October, 1999.

Fenton, Carroll Lane and Mildred Adams Fenton. *The Fossil Book: A Record of Prehistoric Life,* rev. ed. New York: Doubleday, 1989.

Fortey, Richard. *Life: A Natural History of the First Four Billion Years of Life on Earth.* New York: Alfred A. Knopf, 1998.

Gould, Stephen Jay. *Wonderful Life: The Burgess Shale and the Nature of History.* New York: W. W. Norton & Company, 1989.

Gould, Stephen Jay, ed., *The Book of Life: An Illustrated History of the Evolution of Life on Earth.* New York: W. W. Norton & Company, 1993.

McGowan, Chris. *Diatoms to Dinosaurs: The Size and Scale of Living Things.* Washington, DC: Island Press, 1994.

McMahon, Thomas A. and John Tyler Bonner. *On Size and Life.* New York: Scientific American Library, distributed by W. H. Freeman and Company, 1983.

Milne, Lorus J. and Margery Milne. *Insect Worlds.* Charles Scribner's Sons, 1980.

Preston-Mafham, Rod and Ken Preston-Mafham. *The Natural History of Insects.* Ramsbury, UK: Crowood Press, 1996.

Ritvo, Harriet. *The Animal Estate.* Cambridge, MA: Harvard University Press, 1987.

Vogel, Steven. *Vital Circuits: On Pumps, Pipes, and the Workings of Circulatory Systems.* New York: Oxford University Press, 1992.

—-. *Cats' Paws and Catapults: Mechanical Worlds of Nature and People.* New York: W. W. Norton & Company, 1998.

Wilson, Edward O. *In Search of Nature.* Washington, D.C.: Island Press, 1996.

Wootton, Anthony. *Insects of the World.* New York: Facts on File Publications, 1984.

Zimmer, Carl. "See How They Run." *Discover,* September, 1994.

Page numbers in **boldface** are illustrations and charts.

Marc Zabludoff, former editor in chief of *Discover* magazine, has been involved in communicating science to the public for more than two decades. He has written two other books in this series for Marshall Cavendish, on reptiles and on the kingdom of life made up of the chiefly microscopic—and largely unknown—organisms known as protoctists. His books for the AnimalWays series include *Spiders* and future works on beetles and monkeys. Zabludoff lives in New York City with his wife and daughter, who are trying, not always successfully, to share his fascination with six-footed creatures.